Belgian Homing Pigeons: Their Rearing, Training And Management

Hartley and sons

BELGIAN
HOMING PIGEONS:

THEIR REARING, TRAINING, AND MANAGEMENT;

BY

HARTLEY & SONS, WOOLWICH.

A SHOW ANTWERP.

Second Edition.

PUBLISHED BY THE AUTHORS.

PRICE SIXPENCE.

BELGIAN
HOMING PIGEONS:

THEIR REARING, TRAINING,
AND MANAGEMENT.

"Venus, for a hymn of love,
  Gave me to the bard away;
  See me now his faithful minion;
  To his lovely girl I bear
  Songs of passion thro' the air."
                    Anacreon, B. C. 600.

Second Edition.

PUBLISHED BY THE AUTHORS,

HARTLEY & SONS, WOOLWICH.

Price Sixpence.

LONDON :

PRINTED BY CHARLES HOWES,
VULCAN ROAD, BROCKLEY,
S.E.

BELGIAN HOMING PIGEONS.

CHAPTER I.

BELGIUM AND ITS PIGEONS.

F it be true, as is said, that when good New Yorkers die they go to Paris, then surely it may be added that when good pigeon amateurs die, they go to Belgium. For generations the Belgians have been breeding and perfecting homing pigeons, and no one acquainted with the subject would pretend that their birds are not incomparably superior to the native English pigeons in homing instinct and rapidity and power of flight. Five hundred miles is by no means an extraordinary distance for a Belgian homing pigeon, and the following are frequent achievements, viz.:—Lourdes to Liege, 565 miles; Bayonne to Ghent, 560; Tarbes to Malins, 554; Morceux to Ghent, 545; Toulouse to Liege, 505; Montpellier to Brussels, and Agen to Malins, 487; Bordeaux to Liege, 478, and so on. Even greater distances than these have been traversed, birds having been flown from Rome to Brussels, about 900 miles. In one day as many as 50,000 "pigeons voyageurs" have been sent through Brussels on their way to training stages. In bringing their birds to such perfection the Belgians have of course expended much time and labour, and they have had to bear the loss of countless thousands of indifferent birds. The English amateur may profit to a great extent by their experience if he will stock his loft with Belgian pigeons. The writer on "Homing Pigeons" in Mr. R. Fulton's "Illustrated Book of Pigeons," the standard work of its kind, says:— " The long distances attained and the number of birds sent those distances, prove that the good birds in Belgium are legion. * * Nearly all the birds used in England which are of any value for flying have been brought from Belgium, or are the produce of such imported birds. * * From the experience I have had with birds, both English and Belgian, I advisedly urge every amateur to get his birds from Belgium." These remarks we fully endorse. If the pigeon amateur is able to go to Belgium and select birds for himself, well and good; and we know of no more agreeable way of spending a holiday than visiting that deeply interesting country, with its handsome capital, its art treasures, its battle-fields, and many other attractions. Antwerp, to which the visitor in search of "pigeons voyageurs" will probably make his way, is the principal seaport of Belgium, advantageously situated on the Scheldt, with a population of 175,000. It can scarcely be called a handsome city, but its Cathedral is worth a journey from England to see, and it is rich in the master-pieces of Rubens and other great painters. The population is mostly Flemish, and that is the language spoken by the vast majority, but the tradesmen in the principal streets and most other people that the ordinary visitor is likely to meet, speak French. English is spoken at all the principal hotels. The traveller in search of pigeons will have great difficulty if he cannot speak French, and even then he will probably meet some pigeon "amateurs"—that is the equivalent for "fancier"—who knows nothing but Flemish. Inasmuch as our knowledge of that language is confined to "Ingang," "Uitgang," "Verboden," and about a dozen other words that we have seen pretty liberally distributed about the Docks and Railway Stations—and of all of which we are not quite sure that we know the meaning— we have had some very laughable adventures with some of these Flemings, who knew about as much French as we knew of their language, but who would persist in discoursing most fluently, and possibly most eloquently, on the merits of birds which they held in their hands. A neighbour who speaks French, however, is generally to be found to come to the rescue. There are no pigeon shops in Antwerp, but there are plenty of "marchands de pigeons," some of whom supply "good flying birds for the concours" at 9/- per dozen. We believe they make very good pies. Having secured his pigeons we recommend the English visitor to

send them home via Harwich. Even if he returns via
Calais he will find this much the cheapest way of forwarding
them, as the Railway Company will not allow him to take them
as baggage.

This treatise is confined to a particular breed of pigeons,
known under the various names of Antwerps, Homing
Pigeons, Belgian Voyageurs, Smerles, &c., a variety entirely
distinct from the old English Fancy Carrier Pigeons. The
latter are now seldom met with except at pigeon shows, and
constitute an artificial high-class breed, valued solely for
certain points, and which are now never used for carrying
messages or flying matches. The English wattled Carriers
are very difficult to breed to the requisite standard of perfection, and are expensive and troublesome to rear, the
birds being very capricious nurses. It is also desirable to
correct another very common mistake which arises from a
confusion of the numerous names applied to this class of
birds. The name " Antwerps " is now generally applied to
a very short-beaked show variety, bred to a certain standard
of form, colour, marking and points, and is usually of comparatively little value for finding its home from long distances.

The pigeons treated of in this work are a mixed and
composite race, not confined to Antwerp ; but are bred
all over the Continent, in many parts of which they form the
national hobby. In rapidity and power of flying and the
possession of an instinct which enables them to find their
homes from almost incredible distances, they far excel, as
we have said, all our English varieties. These birds are
matched and bred by the Belgian Societies and amateurs
without the slightest regard to colour, uniformity of appearance or points. Speed, endurance, and homing instinct are
the objects to be attained, and to secure these every other
consideration is disregarded. For the information of those
who may be induced under a mistaken apprehension to
purchase them for exhibition at Poultry and Pigeon Shows,
it may be stated that Mr. Tegetmeier (a high authority and
judge at such shows) writes that " It is utterly absurd to
judge of Antwerp Homing or Carrier Pigeons by certain

points or characteristics of appearance, for they have no points or characteristics or appearance that can afford any criteria for a judge to decide upon." This is a lesson which our English friends are slow to learn, for many of them seem to be of the opinion of a correspondent of *Poultry*, who said he would not have an ugly homer at a gift, even if it would fly from the North Pole without training. This reads somewhat like Joseph de Maistre's supposition of the dog which should want to be saddled and bridled to carry him into the country, and the horse which should take it into its head to leap on to his knees or to take coffee with him ; and in the words of another French writer is almost "to wish that nightingales should sing the symphonies of Beethoven." But it is not much use arguing with the people who hold these views, and it is fortunate that many of the Belgian Carrier Pigeons are graceful, handsome birds, possessing more or less of the qualities of appearance which attach to show Antwerps. The most frequent colours are mealy or silver dun, blue, blue chequer and red chequer ; but as the birds are bred for flying and not for colour, they will not always breed true to colour, and the young birds are just as likely to be the colour of their grand-parents as of their parents. In shape they somewhat resemble the common blue rock, but the breast is full and wide, the head broad, the eye prominent and the beak thick. Birds of medium size are usually found best for long distances. In some, the beak is long, indicating an affinity or cross with the Dragon, whilst in others, the beak is short, a peculiarity to birds from the Liege district, frequently designated Smerles. The medium beaks are known in Belgium as Bec-Anglais and Demi-bec, and are generally a cross of an English Homing Pigeon with a Smerle or Cumulet. Some breed a little more to one character than others ; but this does not affect the good qualities of the race, and it may be taken as a rule that length of beak or colour are immaterial, so long as the head is broad, arched and well developed, and the pigeon possesses firmness and breadth of flight feathers, and the eye is full and glistening.

CHAPTER II.

HISTORY AND USES OF HOMING PIGEONS.

HAVING said so much concerning this modern development of the genus *Columba*, we may, perhaps, be permitted to go back a little, and say something upon the history of homing pigeons generally, and the uses to which they are put.

Messenger pigeons have been kept for pastime, use, and profit from the earliest ages, and their history is contemporary with that of man. There are records of them in the 5th Egyptian Dynasty, 3,000 years before Christ, whilst the account of the return of the dove to the Ark is familiar to all. The ancient patriarchs, in their searches for fields of pasture at a short distance from the main body of their tribe used to take Carrier pigeons with them to convey back the result of the explorations. Six hundred years before the Christian era, Anacreon put the verse given on our title page into the mouth of a Carrier Pigeon, and they have been used as love-letter carriers under circumstances of danger and difficulty for thousands of years. Not only in love but in war and festivity they have always played a conspicuous part. Varro, who died B.C. 28, as well as Columella, record that long before Rome was built, Carrier Pigeons were popular birds. At the Olympian games, contemporary with Joshua, they were employed to carry the names of the victors to distant parts of the Empire, a pigeon on one occasion returning from Pisa to Ægina in one day. Pliny records that they were used at the siege of Mutina—Decius Brutus sending messages by them into the camp of the Consuls. Thaurus relates that at the siege of Harlem, the city was reduced to its last extremity (as Paris was in 1870), when a design was formed to avert opening the gates to a remorseless enemy, and intelligence was conveyed to the citizens by a pigeon. The ancient Traveller Lithgow wrote that when the French and Venetian armies were besieging Ptolemais, the soldiers secured a carrier pigeon as it was flying to the city, and that it had a message to the effect that the Sultan was coming in three days to raise the siege. The Christians, however, forged a letter to the opposite effect, let the Carrier Pigeon go, and the city immediately surrendered. During the Holy War, when Acre was attacked by King Richard, Saladin regularly corresponded with the besieged city by means of Carrier Pigeons. Then, as now, their use was chiefly identified with warfare ; but they have been used for many other useful purposes. In the East, including Turkey, Egypt, and Persia, they were used for hundreds of years, for postal purposes, towers full of pigeon holes being erected at distances of every forty miles. In China, and many other countries, they are used in the present day as letter carriers, often doing journeys of (333 miles) a thousand li ; the sea-going vessels also keeping Carrier Pigeons on board to convey letters to the homes of the officers and seamen. Within a recent period, Captain Goulard made use of their speedy flight to assist in the capture of smugglers. Whenever a smuggling vessel left the Continent, birds were despatched to Dover and other English sea-ports with intelligence when and where the smuggling vessels might be expected, until at length the dealers in contraband goods obtained hawks to kill the pigeons. The Custom House officers in their turn getting shrikes which destroyed the hawks, the ocean carrier pigeon service was re-established, and continued till smuggling was " put down."

It is not generally known that the wealth of the Rothschild family is due in a large degree to Carrier Pigeons. Before the French cable was laid, Baron Rothschild regularly used these birds to bring him intelligence of the state of the Paris money market, thus enabling the Baron to clear thousands by buying or selling stock according to the information brought. *Bell's Life* and many sporting papers have used them for many years for bringing intelligence from the principal race meetings, and could always tell within a few minutes when the birds would arrive from Newmarket, Goodwood, Stockbridge, Winchester, Sonthampton or Ascot. The writers of this work, notwithstanding the

facilities afforded by the electric telegraph, use large numbers in collecting information for the papers, the reports
being "manifolded" on oiled tissue paper, folded up small,
and tied to the bird's legs. In this way a column of the
Times may be sent in closely written M.S. by one bird. Re-
ferring to this subject, the following article appeared on July
28th, 1874, in the *Standard* newspaper : —

"PRESS CARRIER PIGEONS.—One of the most curious incidents
connected with modern journalism is the regular employment of Carrier
Pigeons in collecting intelligence for the daily and weekly newspapers.
In the competitive exertions to procure the 'Latest Intelligence,' it
has been found that for short distances newspaper reports can be sent
readier, cheaper, and quicker by Press Carrier Pigeons, flying a mile
per minute, than by the Postal telegraph * * * Being expressly
bred for Press purposes—conveying news to our great cities—they are
not the pure Carrier Pigeon, but are of a special pedigree, bred by
Messrs. Hartley and Sons, of the *Kentish Mercury*, Woolwich, from
prize birds imported from the best lofts of Antwerp, Brussels and Liege
—all 'producteurs' being rejected which have not won a 300 mile
'concours.' Press Carrier Pigeons owe their origin to Darwins's principle of 'natural selection,' or the 'survival of the fittest.' In the
struggle for life in connection with the compulsory flying of long distances, the homing and flying powers of the pigeon are developed to a
large degree, whilst the birds which cannot do the distance are necessarily lost and eliminated. The surviving or winning voyageurs become
thus educated to the highest standard of perfection, and this system
being continued through many generations (the flying distances increasing every year), a race of pigeons has been produced with powers which
a few years ago would have been deemed impossible. Press Carrier
Pigeons, though as a rule only used for short distances, in competition
with the electric telegraph, can be specially trained to distances of 500
miles, and frequently fly to England from Dublin, Brussels, Paris and
Lisbon."

The history of Homing Pigeons would be incomplete, if
mention was not made of their use in war. When field
and inland telegraph lines are tapped, suspended, or destroyed or under the control of an enemy, the service of
these pigeons have been made available for conveying camp
and field despatches, for making known the enemy's
position and numerical strength, to control military and
strategical movements, and to order arms from distant
emporiums. In the autumn of 1870, the national pastime
of Belgium (the long pigeon races from the South of

France) were suddenly stopped by the Franco-Prussian War, the French Minister of War naturally prohibiting the entry of Belgian pigeons into France. At that time there were thousands of trained pigeons capable of conveying intelligence from Paris to the frontier towns of Belgium in five or six hours, and information conveyed by any one of these aerial messengers might have lost or won an important battle, or even an empire. After interdicting their entry into France, the inhabitants of Paris were, in the hour of extremity, glad to fall back on the few pigeons " homed" in that city. We have since seen many of these birds. Some of them were very inferior birds; but they did their work comparatively well. They were sent out of the besieged city by means of balloons made of strong calico, covered with two or three coatings of a varnish composed of linseed oil and a little oxide of lead, and manufactured at the Northern and Orleans Stations. The first balloon sent by the Post-office, or Parisian *Estafette* left on the 23rd of September. Between that date and the end of November, thirty balloons left containing Homing Pigeons, and 200 to 300 kilogrammes of letters, charged at the rate of 2½d. for one-sixth of an ounce. The pigeons sent out in the balloons were freighted with letters to convey back to Paris. The first three birds carried in no less than 1,000 despatches, and some of the post-offices in England and France were besieged by persons anxious to communicate with and send assistance to relatives and friends shut up in Paris. The messages to be sent into Paris were limited to twenty words, for which a charge of twenty francs was made, and so well were the arrangements carried out that the number of letters carried by a single bird realised the large sum of £100, at the rate of one franc per word. The experience gained in that war, and the impossibility of laying telegraph wires that cannot be discovered, has made it apparent that in future warfare, Homing Pigeons will play an important part in the military organizations of nations. At the present time every European country, except England, has adopted the Homing Pigeon as a means of conveying military intelligence in time of war. In connection with this subject, an English military organ, the *Broad Arrow*, writes :—

" Connected with the new citadel at Strasburg is a pigeon-house, with accommodation of the most approved description for 300 carrier pigeons, to be ready in the event of war. Are we in England to rest so well satisfied with the omnipotence and omnipresence of telegraph wires as to neglect entirely the homing pigeon? In Germany, the War Department is wise enough to organize a pigeon-loft in its important garrisons, but in England it is evidently to be left to private enterprise to encourage pigeon-flying in Woolwich, Portsmouth, and Chatham."

We may supplement the above appropriate remarks by stating that during the excitement attendant on the war between two great empires, the War Office seeing the necessity of not being behind other nations, appointed a Committee, including Professor Abel, of Woolwich Arsenal, to experiment and report on war balloons, and their necessary accessories, Carrier Pigeons; but the exigencies of the time having passed away, the Committee have done nothing. We regret that this should be so; for our parts, we should have been glad to have given the Committee all the assistance we could in carrying out an object which we consider to be of great importance. The length and breadth of England is considerably under the distance usually flown by Carrier Pigeons, and it would be easy to train and interchange birds so as to get information from, or send intelligence to, any other military station in Great Britain.

Another means of utilizing the powers of the instincts of Homing Pigeons is the conveyance of messages to and from lighthouses under heavy stress of weather, and in certain circumstances of getting information from vessels foundering, in extremity or windbound. Pigeons can be "homed" to ships, which they will accompany all the world over, for twenty years. When the vessel to which they belong goes down they fly to the nearest ship, and in this way they have made known the loss of ships, which otherwise would never have been heard of. Although we have already briefly referred to this subject, yet the history of Carrier Pigeons would be incomplete without prominent reference being made to the Continental Pigeon Races, or *Concours*. In Germany, Belgium and Holland, almost every town and village has its pigeon club, or societé colombophile. Of the latter, there are between 300 and 400, composed of many thousand members, who organize and fly 20,000 matches annually. As instances of what the Belgian Carrier Pigeons do, it may be stated that in the contests from the Crystal Palace, Sydenham, to all parts of Belgium (with time allowances of one minute for each kilometre in case of pigeons having to fly a greater or less distance than Brussels) many birds did the journey at a uniform rate of fifty miles an hour. A gentleman at Courtrai possessed a bird that flew from Belfast across St. George's Channel, over England, and across the North Sea to its home at Courtrai. *Concours* of of 200, 400, and 500 miles are of weekly occurrence during the racing season, and occasionally races are organized from Rome to Belgium, a distance of 900 miles, the birds having to pass over 500 miles of country entirely new to them, with the Apennine Mountains 7,000 feet high intervening. Very few English amateurs have any idea of the extent to which pigeon-flying exists in Belgium. The birds are sent off, through France, often by special trains, carrying nothing but pigeons, leaving Antwerp, Brussels, Liege, &c., about one o'clock on Saturday morning, each train conveying 500 baskets of pigeons to be liberated in distant parts of France, Switzerland, and Austria. Amongst the prizes offered for competition are services of plate, and other presents given by the King of the Belgians, and other members of Royalty, and an annual subsidy of 1,000 francs by the City of Brussels.

Amongst other uses to which Homing Pigeons are turned, is the conveyance of police "informations" to and from outlying stations, to send messages to the nearest police-station, from detectives out on special or perilous duty, from constables at fixed points, and by the residents of isolated mansions to summon help in cases of fire, robbery, or illness. The following report from the *Times* of July 14th, 1877, illustrative of the uses to which Homing Pigeons may be put, will perhaps interest our readers :—

"A Seventy Miles' Race with an Express Train.—Yesterday an exciting race took place from Dover to London between the Continental mail express train and a carrier pigeon conveying a document of an urgent nature for the French police. The rails, carriages and engine of the express train were, as might be expected, of the best possible construction for power and speed. The pigeon, which was bred by Messrs. Hartley & Sons, of Woolwich, and 'homed,' when a few weeks old, to a building in Cannon Street, City, was also of the best breed of homing pigeons known as 'Belgian voyageurs.' The bird was tossed through the railway-carriage window by a French official as the train moved from the Admiralty-pier, the wind being west and the atmosphere being hazy, but with the sun shining. For upwards of a minute the carrier pigeon circled round at an altitude of about half a mile, and then sailed away towards London. By this time the train, which carried the European mails, and was timed not to stop between Dover and Cannon Street, had got up to full speed, and was tearing away at the rate of 50 miles an hour towards London. The odds, at starting, seemed against the bird; and the railway officials, justly proud and confident in the strength of their iron horse, predicted the little aerial messenger would fail; but the race was not to the strong. The carrier pigeon, as soon as it had ascertained its bearings, took the nearest route, in a direction midway between Maidstone and Sittingbourne, the distance, as the crow flies, between Dover and London, being 70 miles, and by rail 76½ miles. As the Continental mail express came puffing into Cannon Street Station, the pigeon had been home 20 minutes, having beaten Her Majesty's Royal mail by a time allowance representing-18 miles."

Some medical men keep pigeons for the accommodation of patients living at a distance, whilst others send their orders by Carrier Pigeons to tradesmen in a distant town. They are also obviously extensively used as a means of communication between relatives, friends, and branch establishments. For this purpose, for short distances, they form a readier, cheaper, and quicker medium of communication, than by electric telegraph, whilst two or more persons or establishments, each keeping them, can send messages and receive answers at any time. A call-bell may be made to ring (and continue ringing until attended to) whenever a pigeon arrives with a message, and they may thus be made to answer all the purposes of a private telegraph. The act of the pigeon pressing the bolting wire, or passing through the tipping hole, on entering its home, sets bell machinery in motion.

Homing Pigeons also form an innocent hobby for the young, their proprietorship affording an opportunity of fostering in after life the priceless qualities of kindness, good management, and forethought.

Homing Pigeons have been identified with sacred and profane history through all ages. The holiest, most gifted and best of men and women have shared our love for these fascinating and beautiful birds, and have adopted them as a means of relaxation, relief of mind, and health. The keeping of Homing Pigeons is not perhaps the highest of recreations; but minds differ. All cannot adopt books, the cultivation of flowers, painting, sculpture, and the high arts as pastime; but the man, boy, woman, or girl who manifests a taste for the cultivation of beauty, combined with the spirit of utility, as developed in the rearing, training, and management of Carrier Pigeons, becomes more elevated and is all the better for it. In keeping and flying them, they not only afford intellectual recreation; but also furnish a large amount of healthy excitement. We have often witnessed the pleasure of a mother residing at Blackheath, Kent, on the knowledge that a voyageur was winging its way o'er hill and dale, with a note from a child at a school in Malvern, Worcestershire. It is also easy to conceive the healthy excitement in the small town of Courtrai, Belgium, when the sixty-seven members of the *Societé Peristeraphile* and a large number of outsiders were anxiously awaiting the return of the pigeons known to have been "tossed" in London at noon that day. Pigeon flying offers an antidote to many objectionable amusements of the present day, and if there are some people who sneer at the "low pigeon fancier," they would do well to remember that many a working man's home is bright and happy because the head of the family spends his evenings at home with his pigeons, when he might otherwise occupy them at the public house.

CHAPTER III.

HOMING PIGEONS: THEIR REARING, TRAINING, AND MANAGEMENT.

A HOME is absolutely necessary for pigeons, the attachment of these birds to the places of their birth being their distinctive characteristic. After being once homed, they never revert to a wild state. Their natural habits and constitution are in several respects peculiar, and without a knowledge of these, it is impossible to rear, train, and manage them successfully. In the first place, then, a home they must have. Of dove-cots, a great variety exist in different styles of architecture, from the stately old manorial dove-house, to the triangular locker fastened on to outside walls of buildings, or the circular ones elevated on the top of a pole, both of which are unsuitable for the rearing of pigeons, apart from their being exposed to stormy winds, pelting rain, drifting snow, and every variation of weather. In constructing and arranging a suitable home for pigeons, a shed on the ground, with a wire, lath, or lattice work run, to allow them to go into the air and sunshine at pleasure may be made use of. The gable end or upper part of a stable or barn also makes an excellent pigeon-house, a trap or platform being erected outside, whilst many persons construct the space between the garret and roof of their houses into lofts, boarding over the rafters, and forming an aperture, through the tiles, opening into a trap or enclosed area. The pigeons enter their cots either through a tipping or dropping hole, or bolting wire, the latter swinging upwards when the birds press against the wires, and dropping again when the pigeons have entered, egress being stopped by the wires resting against a ledge below, thus preventing the bolting wire from being pushed outwards.

Strong and serviceable bolting wires are easily made with pieces of tolerably thick wire, bent at right angles at the top and held by a couple of staples. Tipping holes are openings, four inches square, in the top of the trap, through which pigeons can easily enter, and out of which they cannot fly, their extended wings preventing them from flying through so small an aperture. The pigeons quickly learn these contrivances, and once learnt will habitually make use of them. An adequate amount of light and unlimited supply of fresh air and clean water are necessary for the health of the pigeons, which are peculiarly hardy, vigorous, and healthy birds, and if their lofts are kept clean and dry, and they can get into the air whenever they please, they are scarcely ever out of health. Birds which have their liberty are much less likely to become ill than those which are confined. The internal fittings of the loft should consist of perching places and nesting boxes. The latter are easily made by procuring a 12-inch board the length of the loft, and dividing it into compartments two feet wide by means of boards of the same width, but about 18 inches long, so that they will project six inches in front of the nesting places. This projection is necessary to give the birds some degree of privacy, and prevent them from interfering with their neighbours' nests. Then, as each pair requires two nests, the partition referred to may be subdivided into two, and a pigeon-pan (procurable at any bird-shop or earthenware dealer, at 2d. or 2½d. each) may be placed in each. The duplicate box is rendered necessary by the prolificness of pigeons, which lay a second pair of eggs before the nestlings hatched from the previous ones are able to shift for themselves. The nestlings must not be able to see the mother, or when the cock is away, they will get out of the nest-pan before they are able to get back again, in an attempt to reach the hen, whilst the latter would be constantly worried and unsettled, and spoil the second pair of eggs. The best material with which to line the nests is sawdust, which will not harbour vermin, and sawdust should also be spread on the floor of the nesting places to the depth of an inch. The whole floor of the loft should be covered with sawdust to the depth of half-an-inch—if it is spread more thinly than that it will be blown about by the pigeons. The incubation lasts from seventeen to nineteen days, according to the warmth of the cot and season. The young pigeons should not be handled before ten days old, when they ought to be gently changed into a new nest-pan, the old one being taken away, and a fresh one with clean sawdust substituted; at the same time the nesting-box should be thoroughly cleaned. Children handling the young birds often proves fatal, and with the exception of moving them from one nest to another, they are much better left to the care of the parent birds, and should not be interfered with. A piece of rock-salt and some old mortar, broken up small, a food-trough, a drinking fountain, and a large shallow pan, available for bathing, and containing three or four inches of water, are necessary accessories to every pigeon house. The food-trough may be a little box with two or three inches slit off the lid ; and the drinking fountain may be any contrivance by which the pigeons may get at the water to drink, without being able to get into it. The calcareous matter in the lime is necessary to form the egg shells. If no old building rubbish is at hand, burnt oyster or other fish shells, powdered and mixed with any gritty soil may be used, grit being as necessary as lime. Instead of using rock salt, the amateur may mix common salt with the mortar to the extent of about 30 per cent. Some amateurs occasionally sift quick lime on the floor of the pigeon-house, filling the whole place with fine lime dust, which causes the birds to sneeze, and gets under the wings of pigeons, preventing the breeding of parasites, and conducing to the birds' general health. The nest-boxes should be on the ground. If placed high, the hens when on the point of laying, or a few days before hatching, will often be unable to fly up to them, while the young pigeons, when old enough to leave the nest, would fall down, and being unable to get up again, would be pecked by the other pigeons, which are always spiteful to young squeakers. It cannot be too often repeated that cleanliness, dryness, ventilation, a supply of mortar, and frequent change of water are indispensable to the successful rearing of pigeons.

Pigeon-houses must be proof against the inroads of cats and rats. Cats, if brought up with pigeons from kittens, will not hurt them; but strange cats are most destructive to them. Cats seldom pass through a bolting wire; but occasionally effect an entrance to the cot through the drop-hole, which should be kept closed at night. Rats seldom attack full-grown pigeons, but will destroy nestlings.

In keeping pigeons, a superfluity of cocks should be guarded against. An odd cock is a general disturber of the peace, persecuting the hens that are mated, and causing disorder and turmoil. In mating pigeons the two birds should be placed in mating cages, made out of a box, with a lath partition dividing the two birds—laths also taking the place of the lid. They should be taken out of the loft, out of sight of the other birds, and placed in a dark place for a day or two, until they are mated.

It being often difficult to distinguish the sexes where a large number of pigeons are kept, it may be stated that young birds are always hatched in pairs of male and female, the larger being the cock. In full-grown birds, the cock's colour is brighter, particularly in the glancing hues round the neck, which is thicker than that of the hen. The breast is also larger, and the coo louder in the cock. In fighting, the pecking of the cock is stronger and more frequent, the hen showing itself as more delicate, and pecking more feebly and less frequently. Young birds are called "squeakers" up to six months old, at which age they are in a condition to mate and breed. They will continue to rear young birds, and remain efficient flyers many years, the usual extent of a pigeon's life being ten or twelve years. They should not be allowed to breed after August, lest the strength of the hen should be overtaxed; and besides, birds hatched in September are generally so weakly as to be a source of trouble during the winter, and are not much good if they survive. If the hens persist in laying after the nesting boxes are taken away, they must be parted from their mates. Breeding may be resumed early in February, or even earlier if the weather is mild. Those birds which are hatched early in

the year are the strongest of the season   The young birds
are fully feathered and able to provide for themselves at
four or five weeks old.   From six to twelve weeks old, they
may be let out as much as possible to fly round and learn
the landmarks about their homes, it being a good plan to
paint their traps or the nearest chimney white, to facilitate
the young birds sighting their home quickly.   At twelve
weeks, their training may begin by taking them distances of
half a mile at first, tossing them up into the air, and leaving
them to find their home.   They should be thus tossed from
various directions, so that they may become thoroughly
acquainted with the environs of their home.   The distance
may then be increased to one or two miles, and subsequently
to 5, 10, 15, 20, increasing by 10 miles at a stretch, up to
50 miles, when the distances may be rapidly extended.
Some birds when first flown, alight on the nearest house to
take a survey around them, but they will very quickly cease
doing it ; and will, after a short time, as soon as thrown up,
commence with a habit of circling round two or three times,
and immediately make for their home.   If a little pains are
taken with them whilst young, and they are taught by grad-
ually increasing stages, they will fly with practised ease and
pleasure from the furthest parts of the United Kingdom.
The education of the birds should always commence whilst
young, their faculties of observation and power of flight
being capable of being highly developed by judicious exercise.   The best Belgian strain will degenerate if the birds
are not trained, and in two or three generations their mar-
vellous power may be almost lost.   At the same time, their
strength and energies should not be overtaxed.   When the
young birds are turned out for exercise, the old pigeons
should be kept in.   Young birds will often keep on the
wing two or three hours ; but if allowed to fly round with
the old ones, the latter, especially if at nest, will return after
a very brief fly, and take the young ones in with them.   In
the Belgian races, all the competing birds are trained and
let off together, whilst in England, unless the number of
competitors is large, they are generally tossed one at a time
at intervals of five minutes.   With regard to pigeons which
have not been previously taught the route, finding their

way home from long distances, the following theory of the homing faculty is by Mr. R. W. Alldridge, of OldCharlton:—

"Mr. Glaisher, the celebrated æronaut and meteorologist of the Royal Observatory, Greenwich, informed me that when over London one mile high, he saw the cliffs of Dover, a distance of 70 miles. Now supposing the pigeon's vision to be no stronger than the human eye, the bird would in time, become acquainted with all the important rivers or landmarks within a radius, say of 70 miles from its home. Supposing the bird to be thrown up at a distance of 100 miles from its home, it would see 70 miles, 40 miles of which would be within its home radius; having flown within its home radius, of course it would see its home, and make for it.

"Supposing the bird to be thrown up at a distance of, say 150 miles, it would make three circles to obtain its home bearings; or to use the French term, 'to orient' itself. Failing in getting sight of its home, or any familiar landmark within its home radius, it would fly in a chance direction an uncertain distance (probably influenced by the wind); failing to recognise any object within its home radius, it would again perform three circles, and still failing to recognise its native locality, it would return to the place whence it was thrown up; from this point it would again start in a different direction, again an uncertain distance; again it would pause, and perform the same system of circling, and, if unsuccessful, would once more return to the starting point. Then it would, if a thoroughly good bird, continue to explore in other directions, until its vision alighted upon some object within its home radius. Finally failing, after many attempts, occupying days, it would become a lost bird, and would most likely find for itself a new home in the neighbourhood of the original starting point. Long distances, as 500 or 600 miles, as a rule, are only attained by progressive training, by which the memory of the bird is educated.

The diagram on next page explains this theory.

"A represents the home of the bird, and the circle round is the home circle, a radius of 70 miles.

"B is distant from A 100 miles. A bird thrown up at B, and seeing 70 miles, would be enabled to distinguish a water or land mark 40 miles within its home circle; flying within its home circle, it would see its home, and make for it.

"C is 200 miles from A, the home. When loosed, the bird, not seeing any known object, would fly an uncertain distance, probably influenced by the wind. It might fly as far as D, and not recognising any landmark, it would circle, and return to the starting-point C.

"From C it would take another direction, and fly say as far as E; still not catching sight of any known object, it would circle and return to C.

" Making another effort to find its way home, it would then fly in another direction, say to F ; here it would circle, and its eye recognising some object within its home circle, it would fly with increased speed towards it, and thus to its home.

D
200.MILES
C
E
100.MILES
B
F
HOME
A

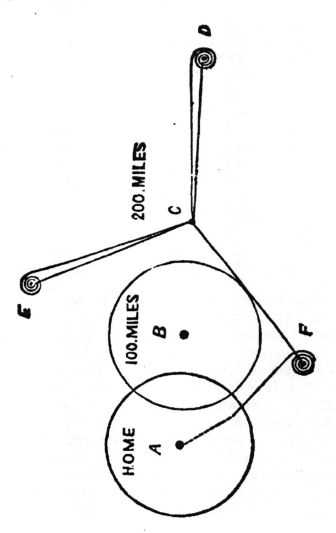

The following table of altitudes and distances, shows the height to which a Homing Pigeon has to soar to enable it to see landmarks at varying ranges. As an example : A bird reconnoitring from a height or building 68 feet high, would see the entire landscape within a radius of 10 miles.

Distance Miles.			Height. Feet.	Distance. Miles.			Height. Feet.
2	...	...	11	65	...	...	2892
4	...	...	24	70	...	...	3362
8	...	...	43	75	...	...	3851
10	...	...	68	80	...	...	4381
12	...	..	98	85	...	...	4946
14	...	...	134	90	...	...	5557
16	...	...	175	100	...	...	6845
18	...	...	221	110	...	...	8282
20	...	...	273	120	...	...	9857
25	...	...	427	130	...	...	11,567
30	...	...	616	140	...	...	13,415
35	...	...	838	150	...	...	15,400
40	...	...	1095	160	...	...	17,519
45	...	...	1386	170	...	...	19,777
50	...	...	1711	180	...	...	22,170
55	...	...	2071	190	...	...	24,710
60	...	...	2464	200	...	...	28,734

The above table assumes the landmarks to be on a level with the sea, such as rivers, large barren plains, woods, &c. ; but in the case of mountains and high rocks, the pigeons would discern them at a much greater distance. For example, a Voyageur perched on a house top in Bombay would see the Himalaya Mountains, 200 miles distant ; but at a height of a mile would be enabled to sight them 300 miles off. Again, a pigeon could see Snowdon from a church steeple in Manchester ; whilst a high-flying pigeon on the wing would see it from Hull. A pigeon on the top of Ben Nevis could see 80 miles ; in the village of Soglio, on the side of Mount Blanc, 100 miles ; in the City of Potosi, in Mexico, 150 miles, and on the summit of the Andes, 200 miles.

Homing Pigeons are chiefly fed on sound maize, small beans, peas, old tares, wheat, rice, with occasionally a little hempseed, the latter being too heating and stimulating for regular food, and only to be used in cold weather, or when the birds are in low condition. Peas form an excellent staple food, and maize and wheat agree well with pigeons in the summer. Mixtures are to be avoided, as they prevent the birds from having a change of diet. Though pigeons are granivorous, they will occasionally eat boiled potatoes and mashed bread. Green food should be provided for them by sowing salad in boxes, and when sufficiently grown, putting them in their cots, or fresh lettuces may be replanted outside their cots. A turf of grass, may, in the absence of better green meat be given to them. When loose lettuce leaves are given they should be hung up, and not thrown about the floor. When his birds are feeding young, the amateur cannot do better than give them for breakfast and supper sound old maple peas which have been soaked overnight, and in the middle of the day wheat, broken maize, tares, or rice. Whole maize and hard peas are very likely to choke young birds. It is a mistake to suppose that pigeons injure farmers' crops. On the contrary, their fondness for the seeds of weeds makes them the farmer's best friends, and they are the most efficient weeders that can be employed. Some of the finest, cleanest, and best corn is produced on farms on which large numbers of pigeons are kept. They cannot root up any sown seed, or peck off grains of corn from the growing ears. They never touch any grain which has not fallen, or been scattered on the ground, and which would otherwise have been wasted.

Pigeons in training for match and sweepstake flying should have constant exercise. A bird showing itself to be constantly distanced should not be kept. Homing Pigeons do not come to their full strength till two or three years old, and if subjected to unreasonably severe distances before their bones and muscles are fully developed, they will at four or five years old, when they ought to possess the greatest vigour be prematurely old and begin to decline. Most trainers have more confidence in cocks than hens. The latter are just as fast flyers as the former; but their maternal duties render them more often out of condition, and hens should not be flown at the approach of laying, or for two or three days following it, and neither cock nor hen should be sent long distances just before, or just after the hatching of their young ones.   In making arrangements for matches, it is in the power of competitors by timely fore-thought to control the time of laying to suit the day fixed for the contest, by taking away the eggs, and so accelerate or retard a new laying.   In catching pigeons to send away for flying, the pigeon-house may be darkened, or they may be captured the night before.   If placed in the dark, they do not flutter about, but remain still.   Some so arrange their cots as to have a narrow space by means of moveable board partitions, into which the birds can be driven and easily secured.   In sending off large numbers, at least twenty square inches, i.e., a space $4\frac{1}{2}$ by $4\frac{1}{2}$ should be allowed each bird.   To ascertain the space required for any number of birds, the number of pigeons should be multi-plied by 20, and the square root will give the length and breadth of the basket required; or to ascertain how many pigeons a particular basket will take, multiply the length and breadth, and divide by 20, the quotient being the maxi-mum number the basket will hold.   For small numbers, say six, the space should be proportionately larger, say 19 inches long, 10 broad, and 8 high.

In commencing to keep Homing Pigeons, it is false economy not to get good birds.   Little reliance is to be placed on merely good looking birds, bred with an eye to fancy qualities.   They should be either trained stamped Belgian birds, or the progeny of Homing Pigeons whose history, antecedents, and performances are known.   It is almost useless to attempt to " home " full-grown birds. They will be restless in a strange place, and ever on the alert to escape ; and some of them, even if confined a couple of years, will be found, at the expiration of that time, able and willing to return to the " old, old home," though it may be 200 miles distant.   We have on more than one occasion had sent to us from Belgium a pigeon which we recognized by our own marks as having been previously imported and sold by us to amateurs who subsequently had let them out.

The greatest care is manifested in selecting the best blood in the rearing of the Press Carrier Pigeons.   The theory that " like begets like," is especially true in reference to the breeding of pigeons of superior merit. Nature has decreed this, and no argument is needed to sustain the proposition as a general truth. If " like begets like," no greater folly can be perpetrated than the breeding of pigeons from the weeds of English and Belgian establishments, or from the birds which find their way into the markets held on Sundays in many of the large towns on the Continent. These pigeons consist almost entirely of voyageurs which have lost their way in long races, or of those rejected by the breeders as slow flyers, and sold as surplus stock. Hereditary trained excellence is everything in getting a good breed, and regard must be paid not only to the intelligence of a particular bird, but also to such facts as the history of pigeon breeding furnishes in regard to the successful union of certain bloods. The Press Pigeons are bred on the principle of " natural selection," or the " survival of the fittest." In the struggle of life, and the compulsory flying of the long distance matches, the pigeons which cannot do the distance are necessarily lost, and are eliminated as imperfect and inferior birds. The surviving or winning voyageurs consequently possess homing and flying powers of the highest standard of perfection, and this system being continued through many generations (the flying distances increasing every year), a race of pigeons is produced of great excellence. In breeding from the best stock, no regard is paid to the fact that birds may be produced at less expense than that attending the use of the most perfect birds, whilst " in-and-in" breeding is utterly repudiated. The in-and-in theory is based on the idea that a preponderance of the blood of any bird of particular excellence, will give to the produce the desired qualities, notwithstanding the infusion of inferior blood in smaller quantities. By an occasional freak of nature, this theory has been sometimes successful ; but as a rule it results in diminished bone, muscle and brain, and we advise one and all never to attempt to stock a loft from a single pair, apart from the well-known fact that he who has a larger number is much more likely to keep them than he who possesses but a few. In breeding, birds of proved power must be matched with birds of like merit, and in no case should pigeons of known good blood be paired with unknown or inferior birds.

If full-grown birds are bought, they should be kept in for breeding, until a tolerable number of young birds are secured. The wings of the old birds may then be brailed or cut, provided their house is on or near the ground, and they may be let out, their inability to fly and the attractions of a mate and young ones, sometimes having the effect of inducing the parent birds to settle down at their new home ; but a certain number, as soon as their wings are grown again, are sure to be off, never to be seen again. The breeding birds, if it is ever contemplated to let them out, should be procured as far as possible from their old haunts and companions ; and for this reason, it is desirable to start with imported birds, the interposition of the German Ocean between their new and native home diminishing the probability of their returning. Another reason for beginning with Belgian voyageurs is that most of the homing pigeons found in England are of a mongrel breed, known by the uneuphonious name of " Skin'ums," generally a cross breed of the Dragon (a good homing pigeon), and the Tumbler (a high-flying bird), or any common pigeon. Though frequently good fliers— more especially against the wind—Skin'ums possess neither the intelligence, nor endurance, nor litheness and graceful appearance of the Belgian Carriers ; but look like the disreputable members of a highly-respectable family, addicted to bad company, and altogether gone to the bad ; and are by no means a solitary instance of how the brute creation may be influenced in nature and appearance by domestication and human associations. Bethnal Green, London, is the head quarters of Skin'ums, where two-thirds of the houses are decorated with a " dormer," or trap, indicating that pigeon-flying is a British sport peculiar at least to that part of the metropolis.

Another mode of " homing " pigeons to a new place, is to get newly-laid eggs of good birds from a trustworthy person near, and substitute them for those of the more easily homed pigeons. A third plan is to procure young birds, from six to eight weeks old (bred from first-class trained birds), and which have never been flown or let out of their cot.   After keeping these young voyageurs in a few days, they may be placed in the trap or a cage, to get familiar with the topography of their new home, and then liberated.   Sometimes at the joy of emancipation, they dart off in a straight line as if by some instinctive impulse, though they have no other known home to go to, and so lose themselves beyond the power of retracing their way.   It is therefore sometimes better to liberate them for the first time after sunset (the chance of their falling a prey to cats during the night being duly considered) and it will generally be found that by morning the impulse to fly away will have gone off.   In this case they will settle on the ridge of an adjoining house, hunger at length forcing them in.   As a rule, however, no difficulty is experienced in homing squeakers, and when they have found their way back into the loft once, they will not give any further trouble.

When Carrier Pigeons are consigned to station-masters to to be " tossed" for training, it is usual to affix on the basket or box, a label as follows :—

LIVE HOMING PIGEONS.

To be forwarded by next Train,

And LET FLY at ....*Station,*

Basket to be returned to ....*Station,*

Please state time of Bird being Released.

o'clock...........*A.M.* | *o'clock*...........*P.M*

The amateur should take the precaution of sending a reply post-card to the station-master beforehand, asking him whether he will be so good as to liberate the birds. In sending pigeons away for flying it is a common error to start them without food, on the supposition that hunger will make them return more quickly. The homing instinct or love of home has nothing to do with hunger, whilst if sent away without food, they become exhausted in a long journey, seek rest on some house-top or tree, and get " popped off " by some rural Johnny Raw, carrying a gun ; or fall a victim to temptation in the form of a plentiful supply of food invitingly laid out on some trap, and when caught, have to undergo a head-and-eye quizzing, wing opening, smoothing, coaxing examination which the trapper always gives a nice-looking bird, in " reckoning it up." The bird thus trapped in the extremity of hunger and exhaustion, if of the right pedigree, is not to be caught in that way ; but will take an early opportunity of escaping, and will ultimately return home, never, it is to be hoped, to be again sent " hungry away," whilst the intelligence of the bird (Homing Pigeons having most retentive memories) will preclude its ever being trapped again.

There is some little trouble, care, and perseverance required in establishing a new pigeon colony ; but this once formed, these birds may be multiplied in unmeasured abundance and unequalled perfection. The lover of these birds has the satisfaction which other bird-fanciers cannot feel, inasmuch as he knows that his little favourites enjoy, in soaring aloft in the sky, that freedom which the poor caged song-birds sigh for in vain.

CHAPTER IV.

THE AILMENTS OF PIGEONS.

The amateur who has attended to what we have said about the importance of keeping the loft clean, dry, and well-ventilated, and supplying the pigeons with mortar, clean water and a bath (daily in warm weather), will not have much occasion to consult this chapter. We may add to what we have said on this subject that the loft must not be overcrowded : and that the perching places should be out of draughts. It is very easy to keep pigeons in good health ; but if they are neglected, they are subject to diseases, of which two at least are very troublesome. Pigeons which have their liberty ought never to be ill. The two *bêtes noires* of pigeon amateurs are canker and roup, and any bird found to be suffering from either of these complaints should at once be isolated. For this purpose it is necessary to have a hospital apart from the loft, but if possible in sight of the other birds, that the invalid may not altogether lose its spirits. If the bird is really suffering from canker or from acute roup, perhaps the best course is to destroy it, if it is not of much value.

We cannot give the reader our personal experience of the treatment of either disease,—a circumstance which we cannot say we greatly regret ; but people who know say that in the case of canker the mouth, in which a morbid secretion appears, should be painted with perchloride of iron, or a solution of nitrate of silver, 5 grains to 1 oz. ; or the matter on the diseased surface may be removed with a sharp knife, and the sore parts anointed by means of a camel-hair brush with glycerine 8 parts and carbolic acid one part. Canker is usually caused by cold or irritation in some form or other. Some experienced amateurs say that short-faced pigeons may get canker by eating dusty food, or living in dusty lofts. Roup, a very bad form of cold, is highly contagious, and no birds suffering from it should be allowed to associate with, or drink the same water as healthy pigeons. The affected bird should be placed in a warm, dry pen, free from draught, and a dose of Epsom salts administered dry, twice a week. The dose for an adult bird is as much as will lie on a shilling, and for a bird in the nest about a third as much, a little more or less, according to size ; or a dose of Epsom salts may be placed in a quart of water, and the mixture placed in the hospital for an hour at 10 a.m. each morning, the birds having been left without water from 5 p.m. Fortunately, however, neither canker nor roup is common to homing pigeons. Colds are easily cured in the early stages by placing the invalid in a warm pen, bathing the feet in warm water for a few minutes, and afterwards well drying them. If the case is a bad one, one drop of tincture of aconite may be administerd—half the dose for a small or young bird ; or the mouth may be washed out with lime-water, purchased from a chemist, and the eye bathed with warm water, and dried with a soft clean rag. Diphtheritic roup is an ailment in which the bird shews signs of cold, and a morbid growth appears in the mouth. In this case, the mouth should be washed out frequently with lime-water, and Epsom salts should be administered every other day. If a pigeon is " going light," its food should be changed from peas, beans, tares, or maize, to wheat, rice, barley without husk, or dari, which are easily digested, with a little hemp-seed. These are the principal diseases to which pigeons are liable. It may be added, in case of accident, that a fractured wing should be slung in its normal position, and in the case of a broken leg, the two ends of the bone should be carefully adjusted, and splints of some soft material bandaged round them. Insects are sometimes very trouble some, especially in hot weather ; but this annoyance may be obviated by cleanliness, the birds being provided with a bath every day, and sawdust being used in the way already indicated. The small feather louse is probably never absent altogether, but it will not increase to a troublesome extent with ordinary care. Other more noxious insects may be destroyed by freely dusting amongst the feathers insect powder, the principal component of which is strychnine.

Having enumerated the ailments to which pigeons are most subject, we can only conclude this chapter as we began, by urging the amateur to aim at the *prevention* of diseases.

Lightning Source UK Ltd.
Milton Keynes UK
UKOW011840290312

189844UK00007B/50/P